Stuck on Yellow

Stop Stalling, Get Serious, and Unleash Your Productivity

Dr. Caruso,
Thank you for the
gift of vision. I hope
you enjoy how I
see the world.

KEN OKEL

ISBN: 0991395107
ISBN-13: 978-0-9913951-0-1

DEDICATION

To my loving and supportive family:
Great people help make success look easy.

CONTENTS

INTRODUCTION

Do you remember the time when you knew exactly what to do when you were presented with a new challenge? You're not alone if you felt overwhelmed by all the thoughts that raced through your mind.

Paralysis by possibility is real and perfectly normal. The problem is that some of us get trapped in this state of mind. You are *Stuck on Yellow*.

It's like when you're driving and you see the traffic light turn yellow. Immediately you are flooded with thoughts. Should I speed up, slow down, check for oncoming traffic, look for a police officer, see if I'm being tailgated, continue to sip my coffee, or change the radio station?

Eventually, you make a decision but it may not have been the right one. What if you found yourself constantly in that state of mind?

Competency isn't the problem. Today we live in the *Age of Competency* where most people have valuable skills and talents. But they don't know what to do when they are challenged by the uncomfortable. How you react to these problems can improve your productivity.

Boosting productivity is about changing the way you think, rather than making a list. Strategic decisions can free up your time and allow you to focus on your big picture goals. *Stuck on Yellow* will give you the strategies and confidence to change.

Before you flip this page, I want you to know how the structure of this book has been designed for people who live busy lives.

As an author, the last thing you ever want to see is your book being used as a paperweight on a desk. Books are meant to be read, remembered, and acted upon. Too often, they become monuments of a busy schedule.

You mean to get around to reading the book but somehow, you never find the time. I'm not immune to this syndrome!

I can't give you more time but I can make this book as easy for you to digest as possible. It's arranged into 26 chapters, each representing a letter of the alphabet and each built around a simple theme that can help improve your productivity.

While you are more than welcome to read the book from cover to cover, it's not your only option. Pick a letter, read the chapter, and consider how you can put the principles into action. Rinse and repeat!

Living a life where you feel stuck is no fun. Pick a chapter, change your life.

"A"

ATTACK OF THE MEETING MONSTERS

Most professionals dream of better hair, a slimmer waist, and shorter meetings. Over time, they learn that the first two are possible but shortening meetings are part of a much larger challenge.

As you may know, the biggest complaint is that they run too long. You sit in agony, for countless hours, thinking about everything else you should be doing. This loss of precious time doesn't happen by accident.

Meeting Monsters are real and they will eat your time. They take the form of otherwise perfectly reasonable, colleagues. Put them in a room, with an agenda, and something happens to them.

The good news is that you can protect yourself from their bite much like how garlic is used to repel vampires.

I've identified six *Meeting Monsters* that eat up time, chew up effectiveness, and spit out more problems. Try at least one and see how it can improve your productivity:

If You Breathe, Then You Must Talk

In some organizations the corporate culture makes everyone feel like they have to contribute to a discussion. Not talking is seen as losing power in the company hierarchy.

As a result, you get people talking who really don't know what they're talking about. While they may mean well, they are the equivalent of a fan of medical dramas giving advice to a doctor.

Create an environment where people understand that contributing to a conversation is welcome if you are adding something to the discussion. Repeating previously expressed points or going off on a tangent should be avoided, unless the meeting has been advertised as a brainstorming session.

The Good Times Gang

These meetings tend to be very fun. People talk about what they watched on TV last night, jokes are shared, and there's much laughter. It's like a party.

The problem is that there is very little work getting done. This scenario is especially common in organizations that are experiencing challenges. No one is willing to make tough decisions or decisions that will change the future of the business. It's a lot more fun to chat about the results of the most recent episode of *American Idol*.

Make sure the discussion stays focused on your agenda. As you are talking, new topics emerge but it's up to the group to decide whether to address them immediately or schedule them for another time. Every item on your agenda needs to either have a resolution or a next step. Otherwise, today's challenge will be allowed to live on for weeks and months.

When I worked in TV news, story idea meetings could be somewhat free flowing and random. By the nature of the work, there could not really be an agenda as news was constantly evolving. In this scenario, creative thought could be acceptable as long as it was focused on producing a news story.

The Artist

This person frequently spends the entire meeting doodling. While everyone is talking about important stuff, the artist's attention is focused on recreating a masterpiece, like the Sistine Chapel, on a legal pad.

This is a distraction. Would you want a pilot doodling while landing an airplane? Put down your pencil or pen and focus on the meeting. There are those who swear that they think better while drawing. This may be true but how does the sketching affect the people who are sitting around the artist?

Imagine that you are addressing a group of people and when you look to them for a reaction, all you see are the tops of heads because everyone is doodling. Does that fill you with confidence? Keep your focus on the meeting and it will move faster. People should not have to wait for an artist to reengage with the topic.

I'll be Right There

This person does not like meetings. Avoiding them is embraced as an art form. The challenge is that the meeting is being held for that person's benefit. The meeting can't move ahead without that person's decision or comments.

Eventually the person will show up, much like a guest might arrive, fashionably late, for a party. "Tell me what I missed," is usually the first thing said.

Then everyone in the room has to listen to what has already been discussed. Some things, like leftovers, are not better the second time.

Make sure that everyone agrees that they will not start the meeting until all participants are there. If someone is delayed or can't make it, then reschedule the session.

Treat meetings like a surprise birthday party where if a guest doesn't come on time to hide behind the sofa, the surprise is spoiled.

Lighting Cigars with Money

Long meetings often become the equivalent of burning many $20 or $50 bills. Look around the room at your next meeting. Calculate how much you're paying people to sit in a room.

It can add up fast. Is it any wonder that you may be falling short of your big picture goals? Instead of chasing them, your team is focused on molding the furniture to their backsides.

If a meeting does not lead to an action or a decision, then it is a net loss of productivity.

Has anyone ever complained that a meeting was too short?

"B"

THE BAD CHOICE BUFFET

In today's pressure packed, ever changing business world, making good choices is critical to your productivity. But you rarely get to make these important decisions in a pressure free environment.

Imagine that you and a friend have just arrived at the buffet of your dreams. In front of you are dozens of foods that you adore.

Everything sounds great but then you're thrown a curveball as you notice the arrival of two full tour buses. Out comes dozens of hungry, competitive eaters. These are people who can consume a tremendous amount of food, like hot dogs, in a short amount of time.

You are now faced with a threat. The hungry, competitive eaters will likely devour the buffet's contents in a matter of minutes, leaving you with crumbs.

If you have any chance of getting the food that you want (and not being stuck with endless iceberg lettuce), you and your friend must quickly strategize a plan that will allow you to get the items you really want before they're gone.

The stakes are high because if you make bad choices under pressure, then you'll never get close to the carving station, the crab legs, or the sundae bar.

While this is a whimsical situation, very often on the job, making an important decision feels like you're at *The Bad Choice Buffet*, where the wrong move will give you indigestion or an empty stomach. Here are some ways you can make better decisions under unexpected pressure:

Know What You Must Have

There is a difference between what you desire and what you must have. You may desire everything at the buffet but there's no way you can eat it all. You've got to make choices or you'll end up with nothing. That's the price of not focusing on what is most important.

On the job, what is your main goal? This is the thing that primarily generates your salary. Do your daily decisions support it?

A decision can be a good one and simultaneously not support your long term objectives. Understand the difference.

Have a Plan

In the buffet scenario, the best way for you and your friend to get the most fulfilling meal is to split up, load up on foods you both enjoy, and then share them. So, one person grabs the entrees while the other stacks a plate full of the sides and the bread.

At the buffet, the competitive eaters are your unexpected competition. In the marketplace, similar threats can emerge. You need to quickly measure the threat and come up with a plan. This may involve doing things differently than you have in the past.

Get Help When You Need It

The alliance of you and your friend may have been unexpected. Typically, you don't enter a buffet thinking of another person's needs. However, you both share the goal of getting the best meal and together you can move closer to that goal that you can on your own.

When faced with a problem, don't suffer in solitude. Find people who can help you come up with a solution.

Pressure is almost always on the menu when you need to make an important decision.

"C"

COULD THIS HAPPEN TO YOU?

Ever go blank in front of hundreds of people? It happened to two professional ballet dancers while performing. They were circling the stage, arm in arm, the epitome of grace and power.

Suddenly "Sarah" and "Mitchell" forgot their next move. Sarah whispered to her partner, "Do you know what's next?"

He whispered back, "I don't remember."

They couldn't figure out how they were supposed to break out of the circling and they were fast becoming like an airplane, winding its way around a control tower, unsure when it will be allowed to land.

This was not a case of normal performance anxiety. Both dancers were in their 30s. They had been dancing since they were four years old.

Eventually, the pair decided their best course of action was to continue dancing around the stage. After a few laps, muscle memory kicked in and they were able to continue the show.

While their fellow dancers and the orchestra were wondering what was going on with the two seasoned dancers, they adjusted their performances to match the improvisation.

Later Sarah and Mitchell, while embarrassed by their confession, were proud that hardly anyone in the audience ever realized that something went wrong. How did they overcome such a challenging situation?

1. They stayed calm. Stopping was not an option for the dancers. They kept moving and honored the audience and the performance.

2. They trusted one another. The dancers put their egos aside and asked each other for help. While neither could deliver an immediate solution, they approached the problem with a united front.

3. They had good training. Eventually, the hours of practice paid off as their memories returned. Mastery of a craft does not mean you are mistake free. Instead, you are able to calmly find solutions to unexpected problems. It's very rare that you see a high performer who panics. Practice gives you a foundation for success.

There will come a time when the unexpected arrives at your job. You will be fine if you accept the situation calmly, have allies who can help you regain your focus, and have the training to find a good solution.

Often our biggest successes are the challenges we overcome when everyone is unknowingly watching.

"D"

DESPERATION PRODUCES
CREATIVITY

If you want to do good work, then you need to get desperate. Yes, living with a sense of desperation isn't comfortable but that's the point. I've learned that desperation leads to creative solutions.

When I worked in TV news, there was always time pressure. It was rare that you'd ever get to do a story exactly as you envisioned. An interview would cancel, a spectacular visual wouldn't be as good as advertised, or you'd have a great story but breaking news would force you to immediately switch gears.

That last option memorably happened to me when I went from covering a balloon festival to the manhunt of a suspect who shot a traffic cop. You need to make quite a mental switch when you must go from helium to high powered rifles.

Camera equipment and microphones can also keep you challenged by unexpected malfunctions or breakdowns. There's nothing worse than having someone ready to give a great interview but the camera won't start.

The pressure to succeed could be enormous. The daily or even hourly deadline demanded results and you would exist in a constant state of desperation. While this was uncomfortable, good work could come out of it.

How? You were forced to find a way to make it work.

You would adapt to a changing story, find someone else to interview, and figure out a way to overcome the fact that half of your video was ruined. Or you would learn to understand your story so well that you could write it faster than you could go through a fast-food drive thru.

My news experiences are typical for the fast paced world of broadcasting. Guess what? The rest of the working world has become increasingly like a pressure packed newsroom.

To open the door to more creative thinking while under pressure, consider these exercises:

Make Quick Choices

Under normal circumstances, it can be very good to take the time to weigh your options. That's very useful when buying a new car or getting a mortgage. Under pressure you don't have that luxury.

Imagine that you need to call your five best clients but you're not sure who they are. Now imagine that your office is on fire and you can only grab five client files as you flee the building. By adding desperation, you've forced yourself to make a quick decision.

Honor Your Muse

When a creative idea comes to you, act on it immediately. In the news business, I learned that there was no guarantee that you'd have as much time as you expected to put your story together. You needed to start writing it as soon as possible.

This way, you'd be prepared if the

unexpected occurred; like breaking news. If it didn't happen, then you'd have more time to polish your story. I learned that waiting until the last minute to start something never serves you well.

Embrace the Challenge

Stop worrying about the specifics of how you got into your situation, how unfair it is, and any thoughts of failure. Instead, shift your focus from the problem to a solution. This is where you stop saying, "It can't be done," and instead say, "What if?"

It's a powerful piece of mental real estate and that's where your creativity can come out. Trust the process and ideas will start to come to you.

You are more mentally flexible than you believe.
Exercise these muscles before a desperate situation.
Master them and become much more productive.

"E"

THE ENDLESS PIT OF NEEDS

If you ever feel like you don't have enough time at work to get the important stuff done, then you've probably fallen into the *Endless Pit of Needs*. This is a real place where customers or coworkers take up too much of your time and you get little in return for your investment.

Often these scenarios emerge out of kindness, which usually is a wonderful quality. However, there are people who are like vampires in that they love to suck away at your productive time until you run dry.

It's not easy to say, "No!" but it is often necessary. Time is a limited resource. How much can you afford to give away? I doubt that unlimited kindness was mentioned on your job description.

Let's examine two familiar scenarios and how you can overcome them:

The Free Sample

Imagine that you own an ice cream parlor that gives out free samples. Occasionally people will come and ask for 10 or more free samples. In this case, the loss of product may not be significant but the loss of time should be a consideration.

Do the freeloaders slow down the line? Does their presence prevent the clerk from accomplishing other things? Or do paying customers not get into a line that was slowed by an onslaught of free samples of chocolate chip, coffee mocha, and raspberry fudge?

In this scenario, you need to respect the definition of "free." Free should not only refer to the price of the good or service but should also apply to the employee's time. If business is slow at the ice cream parlor, then give out as many samples as you like. When things are busy, there's nothing wrong with cutting off a flavor addict after two or three samples.

Are you worried about losing a potential customer? Usually, people who are unsure about spending money with you aren't going to move your sales figures that much. Cut your losses and focus on the people who have cash and are willing to spend it.

Free Training

This situation is very familiar for people who work in an office. You have a colleague who prefers not to learn a process or a procedure. Let's say it's filling out his weekly expense form. So every week, he dumps a crumbled collection of receipts on your desk, looks pitiful, and asks you to make sense of them.

Why are you doing this if it's not your job? Because you're nice, like to help out, and your coworker says he doesn't know how to enter the information into the computer. This person is not a supervisor. You both do much the same job.

Helping out is good but helping out with the same problem is not. Don't let someone treat you like an all you can eat buffet of free help. There are those who will prey on your niceness which results in a boost in their productivity while your output falls.

To change the dynamics of this unfair deal, you need to agree to do the work one more time if he will sit with you and learn how to do it. This has to be a legitimate effort on his part.

If the problem continues, consider bringing it to the attention of your supervisor, ask the other party to do some of your work, or run toward the bathroom whenever he approaches your desk, holding a bunch of receipts.

Don't expect others to value your productive time. They likely have no idea about your workload.

"F"

FIREFIGHTERS AND BABYSITTERS

Do you never have enough time to get the important stuff done? The problem may be that you're always distracted whenever you're ready to tackle your big picture goals. It's a chronic problem shared by many leaders, who find themselves moving closer and closer to *Burnout City*.

Your professional life may have a lot in common with firefighters and babysitters. Both jobs perform very important functions. But they are all about responding to interruptions.

A firefighter courageously waits until the alarm goes off to respond to a challenge. He or she can't get too involved in a project because it might need to be dropped at a moment's notice. It's hard to start things when you're never assured of completing them.

A babysitter must focus on a child. From minute to minute, the child's needs can change. The babysitter can take a moment to raid the refrigerator or talk to a friend on the phone but at any time, he or she may have to attend to the little one or ones. As those with children know, a pleasant game between siblings can quickly turn into an argument requiring refereeing.

If your job involves many interruptions, is it any wonder that you can't get enough of the important stuff done? These are the big picture goals that can help boost your career or get you a raise.

Trying to get important work done while being constantly distracted by little fires and employee meltdowns is like trying to blow up a balloon with a hole in it. Is that your path to career advancement?

What would you give to be at least 25% more productive? If you're willing to change the way you handle interruptions, consider these strategies:

Avoid People

Can you work when others aren't around? While not a long term strategy, a lot of time can be gained by having some peace and quiet. This may involve coming in early, staying late, or shifting your lunch time.

The best thing about this is that there's no one around who will bother you. The downside is that you're now working more hours if your schedule is not flexible.

Be Unavailable

It's perfectly acceptable to close your door or put a do not disturb message on your phone. By shutting out the rest of the world, you're honoring your goals. That's not a bad thing.

College professors do this all the time. They've mastered a system where they have, "office hours," for when they'll meet with students. This limits the distractions that can keep the educators from preparing their next lecture as well as researching and publishing their ideas. Closing your door is a time honored tradition in the academic world.

Stop Rescuing

Do people come to you with problems because they don't know what to do? That's a sign of a lack of training.

This can be easily fixed. Don't shy away from the investment in training, as over time everyone's productivity will increase. Also make sure that the training knowledge is captured in written form or as archived video.

Having to constantly put out other people's fires will burn through your time. Is that how you'll achieve your goals?

Change the Culture

Are people afraid to make a decision without your blessing? While this is unavoidable on some occasions, it's not a good use of your time.

To get over this challenge, tell your team if they bring a problem to your attention, then they should also bring some potential solutions.

This puts them in an active, problem solving mode and you won't have to spend so much time on every issue that comes up. Make this behavior a habit and make sure that it is communicated to new hires.

Success is not about working harder but smarter.

"G"

GULP OR SHOT GLASS SIZED PROBLEMS?

Some problems are the equivalent of a shot glass while others are more like mega gulps. Your challenge is to understand how to address each one.

Do you approach every challenge the same way? This can result in either the big problems being ignored or little ones being allowed to thrive like weeds.

Not understanding the size and scope of your challenges will kill your productivity. To overcome your problems, big and small, consider these steps:

Understand the Impact

A copier being jammed by a piece of paper could be considered a small problem. If it happens frequently then it has a much larger footprint on your life.

Living with this challenge has an ongoing affect until someone either fixes or replaces the machine. The danger is that you can become accustomed to these, "little problems," and forget how much time they eat up.

To prevent this familiarity, imagine that an outsider were to come into your organization, like a visitor to your home. Are there things like a toilet that doesn't flush that would embarrass you? In this scenario, you wouldn't hesitate to address the problem.

Little problems won't bring your business to its knees but they will slow you down. Why allow a solvable situation to continue?

Don't Let Size Intimidate

We tend to put big problems on a pedestal and find many excuses why we can't solve them. The size intimidates us and you may feel like everything else has to be perfect before you can take care of it.

Your doctor is probably familiar with this situation. While there may be nothing more important than your health, going to the doctor when you know that something is wrong can be a challenge. You can come up with lots of excuses why you don't immediately seek out help for what's a known concern.

To change this perspective, add some urgency to the problem. Ask yourself, "How much worse off will I be if I do nothing about this problem today? Am I willing to continue to pay that price and what might I lose if I continue to choose inaction?"

Let your answers help you prioritize the challenges you need to address as soon as possible:

Use the Correct Tool

Too many of us don't use the right tool when it comes to solving a problem. Think of it like trying to use a shot glass to empty a full bathtub. You can make progress but it will take a tremendous amount of time and energy to get the job done.

Sometimes the tool is a matter of people power. In this case, it may be too much, rather than too little. Have you ever had a challenge that required an "all hands on deck response?" While it may be romantic to see everyone focused on a single task, you have to realize that you have most of them doing things outside of their normal duties.

You went for a short term fix, by getting more help. The downside is that your decision could have long term implications in that less overall work gets done.

Why not bring in outside help like interns or temporary workers to take on the challenge instead of having your regular staff drop everything? While there may an initial cost, you won't see the ripple effect of a productivity loss from your team.

Solving problems requires thoughtful consideration and ruthless action. Otherwise, the challenge will continue to live, rent free, on your bottom line.

"H"

THE HAMMER SHOULD BLAME THE NAIL

Good leaders understand that you have to make adjustments to get the job done right. Unfortunately, that doesn't always happen.

Too often, leadership becomes a matter of ego. You push your team to do something that's outside of their expertise. Or you want things done your way and won't consider any alternatives.

The results are disappointing and often require you to do more work to fix or replace the first attempt. To illustrate this kind of thinking, let me take you on a short walk.

While cruising through a neighborhood, I walked into a picket fence. Okay, that's not totally accurate. What happened was that I walked on top of a wood plank that had fallen off a picket fence.

As a helpful person, I tried to pop the runaway board back into place.

It was then that I saw that the nail that went through the plank was barely longer than the plank. No wonder it was falling off as it could barely do its job. I pressed it back in as well as I could but I knew that, before long, the plank would fall again as it was vulnerable to a slight breeze.

At some point, the builders of the fence had to realize that there was a problem with the length of the nail. There was a choice that had to be made. They could either retool by getting the correct size or continue the work.

Perhaps, the construction team had been told to just follow instructions and use the provided nails. Maybe they didn't know enough to question them or thought that the nails possessed magical powers.

In front of me was the reality of their work. No matter how hard you would pound on the short nail, it was not a long term solution for the fence.

To get the job done correctly you needed to retool with a longer nail or a screw. That takes an additional investment of time and the willingness to consider other options, but it results in a fence that will last much longer.

In this case, the leader of the group decided it was okay to continue the work with the short nail.

If a member of your team doesn't know how to do something, doesn't know how to do it very well, or mentions a potential problem, then is it smart to keep hammering on them to perform the task as it's always been done?

Doesn't it make better sense to retool by giving them more training? If that doesn't work, maybe you need to consider taking them off the task and finding someone who can get the job done right.

The solution may have nothing to do with the employees. Have you equipped them with the correct hardware? Will they tell you if something is ineffective? And how will you respond?

It's very dangerous to occupy a space where you tolerate a situation that's not working.

You can't motivate a wrong sized nail to get longer.

"I"

THE IDEA QUARANTINE

Too many leaders demand breakthroughs from their teams but don't want to embrace new ideas. Do you see the problem in this scenario?

The ideas are sent to what I call *The Idea Quarantine.* This is a place where the rejected notions are treated like viruses, sent to die, and are never heard from again. The dismissal is frequently premature. Think of many of the innovations during the past 10 years. Most did not start perfectly formed, yet someone had the courage to say, "Keep working on that."

If you work at Google, part of your job is to say, "What if?" You are paid to think of better ways to do things.

Innovation and breakthroughs take time. You can't expect to use a butter knife as a sword. Given time the metal from the wimpy knife can be folded and strengthened into something amazing.

Does this make sense? Then why do we consider ideas as either being good or bad? Should there not be a third category for those that need some nurturing? Let's change the way your team's mental light bulbs are evaluated:

- As a leader, the next time you hear an idea that isn't quite right, will you take a moment to consider it before you send it to the scrap pile?
- Will you discuss ideas' shortcomings and encourage solutions to the challenges?
- Create a culture where your team understands that "not now," does not mean "never." E-books have grown massively in popularity with the creation of affordable and portable e-readers. Before that innovation could happen, technology needed to catch up with imagination.
- Set boundaries for how much time someone can work on a new idea. It

should be a part of the workday or week but not to the point where it makes general tasks suffer. Think of new ideas like a dessert and not your meat and potatoes.

- Let your team know that there's no shame in throwing in the towel on an idea that just can't be made to work.
- Reward innovation. Any employee can just perform their job, those who go beyond it should be recognized.

Create a culture that encourages creative thinking. When someone feels empowered to pursue their ideas they become a much more valuable employee.

Nothing kills innovation faster than rejection.

"J"

JUNK MAIL OR GOOD ADVICE?

Has someone's advice shaped your life in a good way? That's fantastic, but have you also received your share of bad advice? Even well intentioned advice can take the form of mental junk mail.

We all remember the good advice we've received and perhaps that makes us eager to share our own advice with others. We want to "pass on" the positives.

The result is that there is an all you can eat buffet of questionable advice and you may feel like you're holding an overflowing plate.

Let's get rid of this mental indigestion by considering these factors:

Perspective

If you love cats and I love dogs, do we see the world the same way? The same goes for an accountant and painter.

No one perspective is wrong but it's filtered through a subjective lens. Make sure you understand the other person's world before accepting their advice.

Is it Still Useful?

Sometimes people will give you out of date advice. After moving to a new city, I asked a friend if she could recommend a good doctor. She advised me to visit her doctor.

About three months later, I told my friend that the doctor was not very good and I was thinking of switching to another one. I was nervous about telling her this news.

I was surprised that she told me that she had stopped going to that doctor a long time ago.

I asked, "Why did you send me to a doctor you didn't like?" but my friend only gave me a blank stare in response.

I wonder if it's because we are so excited to be asked for our advice that we feel that if we say nothing, then we'll burst into flames. "I don't know," is an acceptable response.

Need Affirmation?

At times the person who is asking for advice is looking for affirmation.

If I'm asked, "Should I eat nothing but grapes for the next year?" I'm likely to say, "No, eat a well balanced diet." The other person then says, "You just don't understand the grape diet."

So why was my advice solicited? Because someone wanted me to say that grapes are the only food you need to eat. When I didn't, I was dismissed as being the source of bad advice.

Do You Really Need the Advice?

When a situation arises where you feel you need help, try mentally turning the tables. Pretend that someone else has approached you with the same problem. Make this someone you care about and someone who values your advice. What would you tell that person to do?

Once you have that answer, follow your own advice. If it's good enough for someone you care about, then it should be good enough for you.

Toss bad advice in the garbage like junk mail.

"K"

KEEP THE CAN

How can an investment of less than a dollar make someone feel good about spending $250 with you? Do you think that such knowledge could shorten the sales cycle with your customers or persuade people to give you more of what you want?

I was introduced to this productivity secret on an airplane flight. You probably know that in a sea of fees, cramped flights, and frustrated flight attendants, air travel has lost some of its magic.

But when it was time for the beverage service, I got a surprise. The flight attendant handed me the full can of my fizzy drink.

"Keep the can," I was cheerfully told.

I was expecting to just get the usual "Dixie Cup" sized portion. At first, I thought this was a special reward but as I looked around the cabin, I realized that the generosity was extended to all passengers.

A small gesture had a big impact. It made me feel good during an otherwise busy day.

Will getting a full can of a soft drink persuade me to fly on this airline again? It's tough to say. I tend to look first at the price, then the overall flight time with connections. After those things, amenities do enter the equation. Hmmm, I thought. For an investment of less than a dollar, an airline may have improved its chances of getting my return business. That's not a bad return for your marketing strategy.

In a complex, ever changing business world can you pass up anything that can give you an edge over your competition? What if you could easily manufacture these experiences. To create your own "Keep the Can" moments, keep these tips in mind:

Surprise

Can you deliver the unexpected? It's an extra perk or experience you can provide.

Maybe it's offering your clients high quality coffee in a place where they would never expect it.

The idea is that you interrupt people's day in a good way. Memorable is hard to forget.

Create an Experience

Some car dealerships have their customers bang a gong after they just bought their new vehicle. I've seen ice cream parlor employees sing a song whenever someone gives them a tip.

None of these are hugely expensive endeavors. They can easily separate you from your competition by giving people positive reinforcement for their choices.

Exceed Expectations

This one is a bit tricky because it requires you to not just give something to someone. You have to give of yourself and sometimes that requires a change in your business culture.

Do you ask people if they have any additional questions, or are you so focused on getting what you want that you don't think to ask? Do you alert people to a potential problem, even though you won't profit from it? And are you trying to make one sale or get someone to keep coming back, again and again?

When you follow this path, you'll have a chance to take your customers to some amazing places in the world of satisfaction.

Giving the Can is a practice that can boost your profile and your business.

"L"

LOOKING FOR SMUDGES

George the Janitor likes to stare at glass. No one has ever told him to do this but he considers it an essential part of his job. While he may look like he's lost in thought, he is one of the most productive people you'll ever meet.

You may find him in a hallway with a towel and a bottle of Windex, saying, "I'm looking for smudges," as he stares at a window or a glass door.

George has redefined his job to the point that he literally has the most job security in his organization. The office he cleans is spotless and it's because everything he does is built around looking for smudges.

For many of his counterparts, cleaning an office is about getting rid of the mess. For them, that's perfectly fine. People who believe that, "Fine," is good enough are easily replaceable.

George is different. He views clutter like a doctor looks at an infection. He gets rid of it and then makes sure "the patient" doesn't get sick again.

George doesn't look for a mess to clean up. His focus is on keeping things clean. So you'll find him searching out the first sign of smudges.

In your company are you focused on cleaning up messes or are you looking to keep things clean? If you want to increase your productivity, you need to understand the difference.

Cleaning up a mess means that you are always reacting to situations. There is no time for long range planning. You go from one emergency to the next. You come to accept the mess and mean to get around to cleaning it one of these days.

George would say that cleaning up a mess is just phase one. After that you need to make sure that things never get dirty again. George does long range planning armed only with a bottle of everyday glass cleaner.

He knows that on a certain door people tend to leave handprints. George looks for the smudges and removes them before anyone else notices them. George knows his marketplace, anticipates needs, and executes a clear plan of action. He does all of these things without a minute of overtime.

Why aren't you looking for smudges?

"M"

THE MEDIOCRITY SLIDE

Great businesses do not change for the worse overnight; it's something that happens in stages. I call this the *Mediocrity Slide*. For an organization unfortunate enough to tumble down the *Mediocrity Slide*, it will take a very long time to get back to the top or where it was. Once you start to slide, every subsequent mistake moves your reputation down even faster.

As you might guess, great experiences keep people coming back. Poor experiences push customers elsewhere; then it's much harder to woo them back.

How do you respond to the challenges that open the door to mediocrity? Here are some suggestions to keep you either moving up or staying at the top of your game:

Keep Learning

A funny thing can happen when people stop learning. They start to look for shortcuts. These aren't things that boost productivity or streamline processes. Instead, these are things that make the employee's life easier at the expense of the organization.

This cutting of corners can become contagious. People start to say, "Why do I have to follow the rules if no one else does?"

To prevent this from happening, you need to maintain continuous training. Don't assume that people, who know the policies, will continue to follow them. Your customers will notice when they don't.

Some supermarkets use software that monitors the speed at which their cashiers ring up purchases. Employees like this in that it gives them constant feedback. Slow employees can be coached to improve their output and high performers can have evidence of their skill.

Why make such an investment in a supermarket? Isn't advertising more important? It turns out checkout time can be a determining factor in bringing back a customer. What keeps your customers coming back?

Misunderstanding Success

There's an old joke about the journeyman basketball player who makes a rare appearance on the court playing alongside a superstar like Michael Jordan or LeBron James. The superstar scores 48 points. The reserve player scores a basket in the final seconds of the game when the other team is already walking off the court.

From that moment on he talks proudly about the night when he and the superstar teamed up to score 50 points.

While the statement is true, it's not really accurate in that it overstates the journeyman's contribution to the game. The same thing can happen on sales teams where some become comfortable and rely on the success of top performers. It's easy to coast if you know that another member of your team will bring up the average. That is, until the superstar has a bad week, month, or quarter. Then it becomes apparent that not everyone is performing to their full ability.

Evaluate individual performance and not just the work of the group. It's a good reminder that improvement and high performance are expected.

Do You Have a Team or Individuals?

Have you ever visited a busy office and seen a piece of paper on the floor? It's obviously trash but no one is picking it up and putting it in the garbage can. This drives me crazy.

It's as if people say, "My job description doesn't say that I should pick up trash, so I'll leave it for the janitor to get hours later." Meanwhile you have trash on the floor.

Perhaps this narrow vision is a product of the recession, where employees found themselves being asked to do more and more work for the same compensation. It has created silos where people let their anger at a company poison the customer experience.

Remind your team that for the organization to succeed and grow, they must think of themselves as important parts of a whole. In many cases, the extra work that is performed, like picking up a piece of trash, will go unnoticed. But leaving trash on the floor will create an impression on customers.

When performed well, there are no small jobs. All make up a well oiled machine. Make sure everyone takes responsibility and pride in their role.

Most organizations are either going up or down. They rarely stay the same. No matter your position, you can make a daily commitment to the direction.

"N"

NEVER STOP DANCING

How do you react when a mistake happens in front of your customers? Too often, we reach for the panic button. This can be a waste of time and energy.

I received an important lesson in dealing with mistakes from the sixth row of a theater. At the time, I was the Executive Director of a professional ballet company, watching our final performance of *Cleopatra*. This was a lavish show that had received extremely positive reviews.

I imagined the final performance as a validation of the company's dedication to such a complex production. The large set pieces could be changed during an act, allowing seamless transitions between scenes. By the final performance I knew the timing perfectly.

Midway through the first act I knew that something was wrong when a large piece of scenery wasn't moving from backstage right to offstage. It was on wheels and a couple of good tugs should have allowed the stagehands, who were offstage, to make it disappear.

But something was caught on the wheel and it wasn't moving. Unable to pull it from offstage, a member of the stage crew had to enter the performing area to give the scenery a big shove.

This made up a 15 to 20 second delay that felt like an eternity to me. In my mind, the entire performance was probably ruined. The technical breakdown had spoiled the illusion. With any live show, you have one chance to make an impression and it felt like we had blown it.

Everything changed when I realized that the audience hadn't noticed the problem. How could they miss such an obvious mistake? The answer is that the company, except for a flustered Executive Director, was prepared for mistakes:

- The stagehands wear black so it's harder to notice them onstage.
- They didn't panic; they calmly walked out and moved the scenery as if there wasn't a problem.
- The floor manager had the dancers hold for a couple of moments before they started their next scene.
- During that time, the orchestra was able to smoothly stretch the music.
- It also helped, that the performance up to that point had been flawless and the audience was very engaged.

When the curtain fell on *Cleopatra*, not one audience member mentioned the stuck scenery. The only way people would have realized there was a technical glitch would have happened if I had stood up and started apologizing to the crowd, which I was tempted to do.

There was no need for that and that's an important lesson for leaders to realize when encountering public mistakes. They are going to happen but does your team understand how to calmly move on? Do they have processes and procedures to overcome the unexpected?

As a leader, you may feel that you need to

react, apologize, and panic whenever something goes wrong. You could end up making things worse. Mistakes don't need a spotlight; solutions do.

Consider potential customer service problems in your mind and make sure your team knows how to react to them. Like the members of the dance company, you want their training to take over when a problem arises.

Sometimes being an effective leader is about sitting back and letting your team perform.

"O"

OVERSHARING PROBLEMS

Every business has its problems but should your customers be the victims of sharing too much information?

I live in Florida and for those who drive the Sunshine State's roads, you may have noticed a lot of road debris. Unfortunately, that results in a fair amount of flat tires. I recently discovered a nail in one of my tires and went to a nearby tire merchant for some assistance.

While I was the only customer at the business, it seemed like it was taking a while to look up my tire history and give me an estimate on the repairs. While I didn't say anything about the slow service, the clerk volunteered some information.

"We just got a new computer system," he said. "It freezes up a lot."

My reply was a simple, "Oh really," but that was enough to open the floodgates.

"Nobody knows how to use it," a second clerk eagerly added; "Even our IT Department. They were never trained on it so they don't know what to tell us to do when we call for help."

"The big change corporate wanted was for the monitor to be able to swivel, so our customers could see what's on the screen," the first one said while laughing. "So now, we can swivel the monitor to show the customer that the screen is frozen."

I nodded, slowly walked backwards, and waited for my critically damaged tire to be replaced. During this time, I thought about what I had learned from this classic case of oversharing information about an organization's shortcomings. It's obvious that this company is being blocked by several obstacles. If I was in charge, this is what I would tell them:

Loose Tongues Scare People

If something is wrong with the computers, apologize and move on. It's rare that someone wants to know the history of the device, especially when it's bad news.

You'll get extra credit if, when you mention a problem, you also say what's being done to find a solution. The customer wants to hear about results or progress. No one wakes up in the morning, hoping to find out what's wrong with your process.

It's Them Versus Us

Your company culture may be totally dysfunctional, but do I need to know this? People expect an organization to function appropriately. Would you want to go to a restaurant where the chef throws meat cleavers at the bartender?

From my tire experience, there seemed to be a lack of communication between those who think up ideas and the ones who implement them. Make sure these people are on the same page.

Be Relentless In Pursuit of Solutions

The thing that was disturbing about my experience was that an ongoing problem was accepted. Fixing a problem should be everyone's priority and part of every position.

If you are a front line employee, tell your supervisor. If nothing happens, tell him or her again. Yes, you may become annoying but in the big picture, is it better for the supervisor to be annoyed or the customer?

If you are a branch manager and the corporate office isn't listening to you, then change your pitch. It's one thing to say that the computers are not working. It's another to explain how much the problem is affecting customers. Quantify how long the sales process is being delayed and if you think any business is being lost. Make the problem, real, from a dollars and cents perspective.

A smile of sympathy from a customer should never be mistaken as sign of approval.

"P"

PEOPLE WON'T PAY YOU

Do you hear complaints from people who are upset that their careers are going nowhere? They are the ones who never get the promotion or the new job. Why? Often these people have little quirks that define them in the workplace. To make matters worse, they are totally oblivious to them and resent any suggestion of imperfection.

These are qualities or beliefs that can hold back your career. They also are productivity killers. Very often there is little to no awareness of them. Here are a few that repeatedly keep people achieving long term success:

People Won't Pay You for Clutter

Loose papers and files in search of a home do not impress anyone. If you must have them, make sure that none of your customers can see the mess. If you're in charge of a public space, its state is a reflection on you.

Project a clean and organized place of work. Figure out what you need to do to maintain it and then execute the plan.

People Won't Pay You if You're Not a Morning Person

If a morning conversation with you consists of little more than groans and grunts, you've got a problem. No one wants to wait for you to warm up. You need to show up to work ready to go.

If you're tired, go to bed earlier, inject coffee into your bloodstream, or do whatever you need to be awake. Your job is not the place where you wake up. That needs to happen in the comfort of your own bedroom.

People Won't Pay You for Excuses

Unless you're a professional speaker (and I am available for your next meeting), they don't want to hear your stories.

You will face challenges but don't let the story end at failure. Explain how you will address the problem. Problems love it when you throw pity parties because then you're really no threat to them. Figure out what you need to do.

Don't let these challenges become habits. Ask others for help if you're not sure what to do.

"Q"

QUEEN BEE OR WORKER BEE?

The need to help others at the expense of your own productivity can become a compulsion. It can also become a convenient excuse to avoid some of your most important work.

Often these tasks can be uncomfortable, so you welcome the distraction from the mundane. You may not know it but it is possible to be busy all day and get absolutely nothing done.

When I was in charge of a professional ballet company, somehow my duties as Executive Director evolved into filling a vending machine with cases of soda and then collecting the money inside.

The person who had previously done the task had left and others had complained it involved too much lifting. Perhaps to save myself from an avalanche of complaints or to escape my duties for a while, I took on the job.

At the time, I thought that by doing this menial task, I was making a statement that no responsibility was below a position and that everyone should be willing to help out during challenging times.

There was a reality that I was ignoring because while I was handling Mountain Dew, I wasn't focused on my big picture goals. Those 15 to 20 minutes weren't being spent on making sure employees were being paid, vendors were compensated in a timely fashion, and donors were engaged. To get everything done, I'd end up staying late. Over time, that mental mileage adds up.

Was I serving anyone by being a very well compensated vending machine stocker? The machine did produce revenue but not a game changing amount. Eventually, I had someone else take over the job. Another option would have been to have paid the soda delivery guy to do the work.

Let's visit another situation. A hurricane has just hit South Florida and thousands are without power or water. Their perishable food has spoiled. I am in charge of a distribution center for food, water and ice. People would arrive with tears in their eyes as they received these essential supplies. The sites were incredibly busy as power and water can be unavailable to people for days.

While I was in charge of dozens of volunteers, I couldn't physically help them. At the time, my chest was full of staples as I recently had surgery. There was no way I could lift a cases of water or a 20 pound bag of ice.

My focus had to change so that I was a leader and not a helper. I had to support people in ways that did not rely on my muscles. I made sure volunteers were assigned to the proper duties, brought water bottles to anyone who was thirsty, and streamlined the distribution process.

Had I been healthy, I probably would have rolled up my sleeves, jumped in, and started lifting stuff. But would that have helped me accomplish the overall goal of taking a group of strangers and turning them into an efficient relief team?

It turns out that the loss of my muscles didn't matter. The volunteers picked up any slack that my absence caused and the operation went smoothly. I was doing more good by overseeing the process and not being an active part in it.

It's very tempting to want to help your team but consider resisting that urge. To be the queen bee, you can't act like a worker bee.

Not everyone will understand this and you may hear some complaints. You'll hear more if you're not succeeding in your efforts to achieve your goals, which usually ensure that people get paid and your organization grows.

Start acting like a leader and stop trying to help out.

"R"

THE RAINY CUBICLE

There once was a man who needed to bring an umbrella to work every day because it rained in his cubicle.

The water came through a large hole in roof of his office. When it would rain, the man would use the umbrella to keep him and his computer dry.

How did this happen? It all began as a small hole in the roof. The man decided it was easier to put a bucket under the drips of water than to talk to his supervisor about the problem.

Over time, the hole grew and the falling water outgrew the bucket. The man finally talked to his boss about the water.

The boss then left a voicemail about the problem with the building supervisor. Unfortunately, that person had just left on a two week vacation. Meanwhile, the leak continued to grow.

When the building supervisor was able to survey the damage, he realized that much the roof would need to be replaced. To get the money, he'd have to have the work approved by the CEO and his leadership team.

That group, while discussing the damage, became sidetracked in a debate about the color of shingles that should be used in the repairs. There is no consensus on a color and the entire issue is tabled.

The whole time, the hole in the roof continues to grow and no one has thought to put a tarp over it. Why would they as there is not a line item in the budget for tarps. Meanwhile the man starts to use an umbrella at his desk.

This story, while not based on a particular incident, may hold some truth for many of you.

Different parts of an organization perceive problems in different ways. Here are some of the challenges that prevent solutions from happening:

Don't Let Problems Stick Around

It can be easy to accept and ignore problems. Had the employee immediately spoken up about the hole in the roof, it could have been addressed faster.

His decision to ignore something that was clearly wrong came with consequences. Make sure your team is empowered to speak up when they see a problem

Is Urgency Shared?

While busy, leaders need to make sure that they are listening to feedback from employees. Employees need to make sure that they are not just dumping problems on their supervisors. Bringing a potential solution can help a leader make a faster and more effective decision.

Personal Responsibility Solves Problems

How would the hole have been addressed if the building manager had considered the possibility that a crisis could happen while he was on vacation? Leaving a voicemail that only states your absence is not a solution to a problem. Leaving information on the message about who to call in your absence, empowers the caller.

Should the supervisor have considered the lackluster voicemail an acceptable response to a problem? And should the employee not have followed up more when it was apparent that the growing hole in the roof was not being addressed?

A Temporary Solution Beats None

A tarp, while not an elegant solution, can be an effective one when dealing with a roof. It gives you time to work out a permanent fix. That's when cosmetic issues can be discussed. It can be very easy to get lost discussing things like shingle colors to the point that hole in the roof is forgotten.

It's a lot cheaper to buy a tarp than a large section of roof.

In many cases the problem is not really the problem. Instead it is the lack of actionable solutions.

"S"

SITTING NEXT TO THE TRASH

The designers of American airports might be surprised to learn that many travelers want to sit next to the trash. For years, the designers agonized over creating as much seating as possible in a terminal and giving people pleasant views while they waited for their flights.

This philosophy fit for many years but has since been turned on its head by a small feature that was once only used by a cleaning crew. I'm talking about the electrical plug.

Our abundance of electronic devices that need recharging has travelers sitting on hard, dirty floors, sometimes right next to the trash. It's where the plugs are located, so it's where you'll find them. For these travelers, having access to electricity is critical. These plugs are hot real estate and folks are proud to stake their claim on one of them.

The designers did nothing wrong when they originally created the terminals. But the needs of travelers changed.

There's a customer service lesson here that can apply to any business. Getting and retaining happy customers helps your bottom line. You may think that you know what people want but that may have changed. Let's push away some old ideas:

The New Most Important Thing

You can have the most comfortable chair in the world but if people value electricity more than comfort, they'll go for the voltage.

Take a moment to consider your attractive features and see if they are still valued. For instance, for years there was nothing wrong with big cars that were gas guzzlers. Then the price of oil went up and the cars became less attractive. The big cars didn't change but the marketplace did. What are your gas guzzlers?

Embrace the Change

Smart airports are redesigning their terminals with power outlets as centerpieces. Seating is built around the plugs or extra outlets are added to existing seating.

If your customers need something different, figure out how you can give it to them. Years ago, fast-food restaurants realized that there was a segment of the market that wanted their food but didn't want to get of their cars. So the drive thru was invented.

Consider New Opportunities

There are some people who really want to recharge their devices but don't want to sit on the floor or next to trash. They need a new solution to the problem.

It has emerged in some airports with businesses that offer rapid charging stations. You pay to have your device quickly charged like you pay to get your stomach recharged in the food court.

This is a simple but important service that shows that people will sometimes pay for things that are otherwise free. Think about how you can offer a service that people want but don't want to do themselves.

Look at the world of pets. Businesses have emerged that do everything for you from walking an animal to cleaning your yard of any droppings.

Don't be surprised if what your customers want may one day change. Meeting those needs can give you a tremendous competitive advantage.

"T"

TEAMWORK: HITTING
THE RIGHT NOTE

Can the success or failure of an organization be due to the actions of one person? Can one mediocre performer negate the efforts of your stars?

As someone who speaks to audiences about changing how they approach challenges, I'm conscious of the importance of preparation when it comes to having a successful performance. It's about doing things that will put you in a mindset where you can just flow with the action. I know my material, I know my audience, and I shape my talk to fit their needs.

I'm always curious to find out how other performers prepare themselves for a show. Once, after enjoying a performance of the North Carolina Symphony, I asked one of the musicians how she gets ready for a concert.

The violist surprised me by saying, "I don't do any house cleaning or anything that would tire out my arms on the day of a performance."

What could housework have to do with musical success? Playing a viola in an orchestra for a roughly two hour performance is a strenuous endeavor. For her, preparing for success, means making sure her arms are fresh. She knows that tired arms create an obstacle to achieving her best work.

Would anyone in the audience know if she had painted a bedroom on the day of a performance and didn't have fresh arms? That could be the difference between a world class orchestra and a nice local music group.

For an orchestra to reach its maximum potential, every one of the more than 50 instruments must be played to its highest level. While some parts are of a higher profile than others, each musician must do everything possible to support the overall sound.

The artists are paid to perform and they make sure they are as prepared as possible. That can mean giving up things to be at your best.

In your organization, do your employees take a similar attitude to work? When they reach their desks, are they focused on the day ahead or are they still recovering from the night before or the weekend? Can they apply some of a musician's discipline to their jobs?

In an orchestra, a principal performer gets the solos. It's a high profile gig that recognizes talent. The players behind the soloist are also very important to the overall sound of the orchestra.

Do the supporting members of your team think of themselves as playing an essential role in the overall output of your organization? Or do they take it easy, relying on the brilliance of your top performers to carry the tune? Do they feel like their contributions don't matter or are unnoticed?

I frequently see this where a company has a brilliant sales team but an awful customer service department. You buy because someone made you feel inspired but later rule out the company for future business because the customer service experience left you frustrated.

That's an out of tune business. It's like the wrong note coming out of the symphony.

As a member of your organization, do you assume that everyone knows their role and the importance of it? Like a conductor are you promoting them to stay in tune with everyone else?

Successful organizations are in perfect harmony.

"U"

THE UPHILL CLIMB

Leadership is easy until you're faced with a challenge. Often, the actual challenge is not that important. How you respond to it will define your success as a leader.

Think of it like riding a bike and suddenly hitting a steep hill. You were enjoying a ride and suddenly, everything changed.

Growing up in Ohio, I got my first bike when I was six years old. It was great to have a mode of transportation that I could control. But taking any trip from my home meant immediately being challenged by one of several hills.

You'd feel your legs pumping but your speed

would start to slow. If you calculated things right, you could make it to the top. If you didn't, you'd have to jump off your bike and walk it up the rest of the way; something that didn't seem too cool.

Responding to the challenges you face as a leader, are just like those hills my little body learned to conquer. Let's replace of some of the limiting thoughts that are slowing you down:

Build Up Speed

As a kid, I knew that if I pedaled fast before I reached the hill, my momentum would help carry me up it.

As a leader, what can your team do to prepare for the challenges you face? If it's deadlines, then can you make a commitment to getting everyone to start earlier? It's about supporting people and not just saying, "Start earlier."

Is there a process that slows things down? For instance, if ten people need to approve something before it can be done, are you really committed to quick decisions?

Change the Game

If I was pedaling up the hill and felt my speed dropping, I would stand on the bike in order to bring some extra power to my legs. Just because I started the hill seated, didn't mean I had to stay that way.

What can your team change that can give them more "power" when they need it? It could be as simple as free or extra coffee during your busy season.

Maybe you need to bring in additional staff or transfer staff to where they are most needed most during your busiest times.

The key is realizing that you can change things to meet challenges.

Focus on the Top, Not the Climb

When you climb a hill on your bike, the more you think about the climb, the more control it has over you. It's much better to think about how you'll feel when you reach the top. It's a mental trick but it works.

On the job, if all you see are struggles ahead, then is it not surprising that your mood may darken and your productivity plummets.

Make sure that your team members understand what happens when they reach "the top." For mountain climbers, the view makes the climb worthwhile.

Consider Santa Claus. Delivering many packages, in a short amount of time, is not easy. But he and his elves know the joy that their efforts will produce when the gifts are opened.

Learn to communicate the importance of increasing your market share, hitting a new customer service goal, or speeding up production. Focusing on those outcomes will distract from the hard work needed to conquer your hill.

Ever notice that the hills from our childhood are not as big as we remember.

"V"

V.I.P. OR F-K

You can waste a lot of time performing damage repair for silly, easily preventable mistakes. These problems cost you customers.

These little mistakes can happen easily but are nearly impossible to overcome. The following story is true. In case you're wondering, surprisingly, no one was fired.

Imagine a fundraising lunch for a respectable nonprofit. The organizers want this event to be the epitome of class and style. Hundreds of people arrive at the attractive venue. They line up at a registration table to find out where they'll be sitting.

The names are arranged alphabetically and that's ground zero for the problem. You need to understand that the cards are divided into four equal sections by letter. Each section is indicated with a sign that gives the range of letters for that grouping.

The first section is for those with last names that match up with the letters, "A" through "E." The sign says, "A-E."

The next group is for the letters, "F" through "K." Do you see how this might be a problem? You see, the sign says, "F-K."

For the pure of heart, this may mean nothing to you and that's great. But for some, it suggests a four letter word.

You have people who paid hundreds of dollars to attend your event and their first brand experience is "F-K." And yes, the mistake was noticed.

While it gives me a good belly laugh, this is a common problem for busy organizations. There are so many things to do for such a big event that you don't take a moment to step back and see an obvious mistake.

The staff member had been given the task of dividing up the attendee list into four equal groups by letter. That person was in a hurry.

While the job was done in this case, it needs

to be about more than just completing the work but also reviewing it.

When you rush, you don't take a moment to look at the sign and decide that the letter range might be less controversial if it was reworked as "E-K."

When people are under pressure and in a hurry, they start making mistakes. It could be a sign, a decimal point on an invoice, or a phone message sent to the wrong extension.

As a leader, you need to get your team to slow down from time to time. Some may feel this will hurt overall productivity. Your team needs to understand that preventing mistakes takes a lot less time than fixing them later.

Otherwise you'll be like the student who only cracks the text book open on the night before the big test. Sometimes you'll get lucky and barely pass. But is this the best way to get an education?

Protect your team and protect their time so silly mistakes won't define your organization.

"W"

WORKPLOSION

A *Workplosion* happens when you're suddenly deluged by an unexpected amount of work that's on top of your regular duties. This scenario can happen when someone leaves an organization or goes on vacation, when downsizing occurs, and when you've shown yourself to be competent and thus deserving of more work.

You feel overwhelmed, stressed out, and trapped by your job. How do you dig yourself out from the rubble of responsibility?

To beat this challenge, you need to be strategic as well as honest with yourself:

The Time Trap

You may feel that the only way you can catch up with all of your work is to put in extra time. This can be a successful strategy in limited doses but the more you do it, the more addicted and tired you'll become. You'll start making mistakes because you're no longer sharp.

Remember, the Greek messenger Pheidippides, who is credited with running the first marathon, died shortly after covering such a long distance without taking a break. Pushing yourself is good but you have to know your limits.

Prioritize the Work

An unending to-do list needs structure and order. Invest the time in figuring out what's most important. Then do those tasks first; this is an important bit.

It can be easy to only focus on the easy tasks or the low hanging fruit. While it's fun to check these items off your list, they may not be the best use of your time.

Ask for Help

Just because you've been assigned work doesn't mean you have to be the person who does it. It's very likely that no one else in your organization knows just how much is on your plate. Don't expect spontaneous mind reading from everyone in your office.

If you can tell that the quality is going to suffer or the task won't get done, you need to seek out assistance. You may not always get help but you won't receive any if you never ask for it. Don't let your ego undermine your performance.

Is It a Trend or a Habit?

A certain amount of *Workplosions* can be expected in any career. If they become commonplace, you need to evaluate your options.

While today's economy may not make you bold, your boss needs to know about this challenge if it becomes the norm.

Sometimes all you will receive is sympathy but you also give your supervisor the opportunity to shift some of your responsibilities to someone else. When all you're doing is struggling to keep up with your work, you may never conceive that there could be another way to get the job done. It's a common trap.

If your situation shows no sign of improvement, you need to either seek out more compensation or start looking for greener pastures elsewhere.

For negotiation, estimate your value to the organization with the cost of replacing your position and losing your experience. This is a much stronger point than saying that you work too hard.

Some jobs carry murderous demands but are a necessary stepping stone to better positions. If this is the case, then put in your time and plan your next move. If you can survive repeated *Workplosions*, you probably are someone who has a lot of talent.

> *In many cases, talent does not determine your success. A good strategy will.*

"X"

X-RAY VISION AND
HIDDEN TALENTS

Did you know that Superman had a boss? Perry
White, Editor of *The Daily Planet* newspaper,
was Clark Kent's boss.

We know that Superman and Clark Kent
were the same person, so I feel safe in saying
that Superman had a boss.

Of course, Perry White wasn't able to
imagine his eyeglass wearing, mild-mannered
reporter as a superhero in tights.

What if he had known? I'm not talking about
revealing the Clark Kent's secret identity to the
world but rather better using his talents at the

newspaper. *The Daily Planet* could have benefited from this knowledge.

Who needs to worry about travel expenses for Clark Kent, if Superman can just fly to out of town stories? White could have gotten better news coverage by not sending Clark Kent and Lois Lane to the same breaking news events. Heck, the newspaper could have saved money by not having to give Kent employee benefits like health care.

I admit these are silly examples but is there a chance that many of your employees have talents that you're not aware of? You don't need x-ray vision to see them. You do need to dig a little.

Is it possible that some of your employees have a secret identity or talents that weren't unmasked by the job application process? At a time when organizations are living in a world of downsizing, it might be a good idea to survey your team and find out if they have any unused skills that could help boost productivity.

Too often, leaders immediately assume that there's no one within the business that has untapped skills. This leads to outside help being brought in at a high expense. Hiring freelancers and consultants can be very productive but it's often better to get someone, with the skills and who also knows your firm's culture and values.

If you do find some superheroes within your business, be cautious about giving them more work. Consider adjusting responsibilities or giving them additional compensation for extra duties. Most people like to showcase their talents and be recognized as being more than just their current job description.

Smart leaders realize that people are rarely just one thing. Embrace all of their qualities.

"Y"

YOUR MOST IMPORTANT THING

It's very likely that you're losing sleep over situations your customers don't care about.

When I was in the TV news business, the big thing was making sure that your station had a breaking story first. Coming in second or third was a source of shame.

I remember people holding legal pads, standing in a panic in front of four TVs, watching and taking notes on all the simultaneous newscasts. They lived in fear of not having a story first.

This was seen as the metric of success. If your station got beat, it was like the locker room after your team just lost the big game.

This is where reality often left the newsroom. It was rare that one station really scooped the other. One might have covered the story better but usually everyone would have something on it. Even if your station was totally beat on a story, with a few frantic phone calls you could put a shortened version of the story on the air before the end of your newscast.

Another thing to consider was that only news people watch four or five stations at once. The folks at home may have made their viewing choices based on nothing more than liking one of the anchors or a respective hair style.

Some would watch your newscast simply because they were too lazy to change the channel after the previous program ended. To them, the claim of having a story, "First," was not going to change their viewing habits.

In today's online world, having a story first continues to be a big deal. Do you, as a viewer care? Has it changed your viewing patterns and do you keep a scorecard at home?

A false sense of reality has been created in newsrooms. The pressure to break the story first has resulted in inaccurate reporting, where speed trumps good journalism. That's something that will cost you viewers.

So we have an industry that is sweating bullets based on something it thinks is important but really isn't. Sound familiar?

Does management at your company freak out if the competition underprices you by a few dollars or opens a few minutes earlier on Black Friday? While these may be very visible differences, you need to step back and decide whether these are issues that really are important to your customers.

Too often, well thought out strategies are undermined in a panic. If you do this, you may be nothing more than a lemming happily running off a cliff.

Slow down, calm down, and decide what really matters in the long run.

"Z"

THE ZONE OF SELFISHNESS

It probably goes against everything your Kindergarten teacher ever taught you, but you need to get more selfish on the job. Why do you need to become concerned chiefly with your own personal profit or pleasure? For survival and growth.

In a complex, ever changing business world, it's not a bad idea to look after your own interests. Surprisingly, these will often match up with a company goal.

Why aren't you doing these things right now? Because you've become addicted to helping out.

If the idea of being more selfish on the job makes you nervous, then give yourself a pat on the back. Anyone who is truly selfish, wouldn't react that way. So, you're still a good person but I'm guessing that your efficiency needs a boost because you probably feel like you never have enough time to get the important things done.

Don't worry, being more selfish doesn't mean you have to be rude or mean to people. Think of it like giving yourself a fair advantage; it's one that can help move your career arc in the right direction:

Honor Your Responsibilities First

Do the job that you're paid to do. This honors your primary responsibilities. If you have extra time, then help out other people with their projects. Or see if you have a skill that you could contribute during your downtime.

You may wonder why you shouldn't drop everything when someone needs assistance. Only you can answer this question, as you know your work culture, but is helping out something that will increase your pay? Will others help you if the situation is reversed?

These answers should define your "helping"

philosophy and not the need to be liked. You shouldn't have to subsidize other people on the job.

Protect Your Time

When did closing your door become a bad thing? If being unavailable is what you need to accomplish your goals, then do it. Most problems can wait and I've been told that email and voicemail are useful tools for those with the courage to wait.

Prioritize

In many businesses, there are opportunities to serve on committees, in and out of the office. Often, they involve doing nothing more than scooping ice cream and blowing up balloons.

While you may be tempted to pursue these extra duties, is your professional goal to put on birthday parties or join the circus?

If the committee doesn't add to your performance or open networking doors, then why do it? There are some exceptions as some people are asked to serve on committees as a way to develop leadership skills.

Most of the time, you're sitting around a table with a bunch of people talking about sandwiches and cookies. Will a superior knowledge of either allow you to get a promotion or a raise?

Time spent outside your regular duties is time that's not going toward your goals. No matter how fun it may be, don't be the first to volunteer for everything.

> *It can be tempting to put your professional needs second to others. Being a little more selfish can mean a lot more for your future.*

ABOUT THE AUTHOR

Ken Okel laughed years ago when a potential employer described him as being "too versatile," to hire. Rather than run from this title, he's embraced it.

For more than a decade, TV audiences watched Ken on the news. At several stations, they saw him perform as a TV news anchor, a reporter, a (pretend) weatherman, and even a talk show host. Ken covered natural disasters, school shootings, and thriving businesses.

He also had some fun as he met celebrities, found out what makes unforgettable people tick, and was paid to do things like free fall 70 feet, ride through the streets in a motorized armchair, and be safely attacked by a police dog. Along the way, this journalist picked up a few honors.

Ken then moved into the nonprofit world for several adventures. These saw him do everything from running a professional ballet company to organizing more than 100 hurricane relief volunteers. Through it all, he understood the value of helping those in need.

Today people know Ken for his leadership presentations to companies and associations. Audiences are engaged and entertained as they receive the tools necessary to transform their professional lives. Some are fortunate enough to take part in Ken's famous paper hat exercise.

People around the world listen to his award-winning podcast, *The 2 Minute Takeaway*. Ken is also known for his weekly column, *The Whiner of the Week.*

Ken currently lives in Florida where he's able to pursue his love to photography, cooking, fitness (because of the cooking), and becoming even more versatile. To learn more about Ken or to bring him to your next meeting, visit www.KenOkel.com or call 561-737-4321.